CRUISE CONTROL:
a theogony

CRUISE CONTROL:
a theogony

by Ken Howe

Nightwood Editions
Roberts Creek

Nightwood Editions
R.R. #22, 3692 Beach Avenue
Roberts Creek, BC
Canada V0N 2W0

We gratefully acknowledge the support of the Canada Council for the Arts and the British Columbia Arts Council for our publishing program, and the Saskatchewan Arts Board for the support of this project.

Edited for the house by Silas White
Cover painting: "Migration No. 2" by Otto Rogers, 1958
Oil on masonite, Saskatchewan Arts Board Permanent Collection
Author photograph by Brad Martin

National Library of Canada Cataloguing in Publication Data

Howe, Ken, 1960-
    Cruise control : a theogony / by Ken Howe.

Poems.
ISBN 0-88971-186-0

    I. Title.
PS8565.O8558C78 2002   C811'.6   C2002-911040-8
PR9199.4.H69C78 2002

In Memoriam:
Clint Morrill (1970-2002)

CONTENTS:

A Pastoral Theology of Cruise Control

That Particular Materiality and Placeness or Situatedness

Stations of the Highway

Guest Speakers

Unproductive Capital

A PASTORAL THEOLOGY OF CRUISE CONTROL

The Surplus Value of the Night

Unhappy consciousness of fore-sleep, in the dismal night
when my eyes, inflated like weather balloons, wander
from their sockets to glide up,

up,

up,

into the silver maple which cups
the streetlamp so delicately against
the few stars powerful enough to

penetrate the city's nyctanthous
veil, while the sore throats of outboard motors mount
the incline of Woodmount
with the slow persistence

of a Business Council on National Issues.
Steam is rising from strings of mycelium, agaricus and coprinus,
fingering the front yard's muddy ooze
and the drone of the heat fills my limbs with a false

claudication, silt from that
"sluggish river of despair that winds dimly
through the porous understory of our most bright and
unprepossessing days." In the night
there are, of course, "tears."

Cruise Control: Calgary to Vancouver

Ignition.

Inevitable as dancing to
"I wouldn' wanna lose yer love,"
the world is falling,
                          falling
along a long road,
in a grey Ford pickup truck
with cruise control, tach, and optional vinyl.

Yoked to the setting sun
which redefines, laterallizes the perpendicular
                                          we are
falling—a cascade of pistons, plugs
filaments, frame, side panels, blood, bile
                                          and window glass.

Plummeting
through harp strings of sunlight—
the beaten gold of the Stoney Reserve at Morley,
the peaks of Cascade and Bourgeau,
the Great Divide and the Roger's Pass,
      the pig's tail cliffs at Golden
      and the sleek shoulder of the Coquihalla Expressway
            plunging
                          into the coming night
                          like a bucket unravelling
                                      into a well without bottom.

We're on cruise control
and vertigo has overwhelmed us,
                              falling

as if the sudden moment before sleeping were stretched,
and transformed into steel and glass and aluminum,
splashed with the smell of the rainwashed highway
liberated by a 385 V8,

released, finally, from inhibition, from hesitation—
        there are no impediments, no
        longer any impediments to our descent.

Hours ago, looking down over the cliff-edge of Calgary
we slipped, falling into the dissolution of civilization,
at terminal velocity.
Cruise control, all the way to Vancouver—
highbeams rake the night, the stars implode,
our pickup truck, gasping, transects the polar
vortex of the sky, drawn by the sunset,
annealed across Yoho,
the Okanagan, Hell's Gate,
by a primal will for motion,
an apotheosis embodied
                        in cruise control.

Self-abandonment is a song of reconciliation,
to nature,
the setting in motion of an uncontrollable descent,

down onto the ghostly mountains, the Pacific,
the distant and invisible lights of Vancouver.

For just as nature is inexorable
so, suddenly, are we,
for that which exists, moves,
        and we are motion,
like this pickup truck, its twin I-beam front suspension,
its fuzzy dice, its Playboy air freshener,
like a rock, oh, like a rock,
echoing the ululation of the valleys,

our ecstatic future sizzling through the axles,
gathering in frame and chassis.

It is Consciousness the
        root of evil,
        the retired judge who
        erects trade barriers, regulates commerce,
        organizes labour, taxes stock options,
        while all around the night rushes innocently by,
        speedometer needle hovering at the speed limit of time,
        its velocity, its trajectory determined
        by a topography, a Ding an sich beyond our

apprehension. Individual wheels may falter,
turn off at some dark and humid corner in the eternal mist
     of the Coastal Mountains
even as time runs on, guiding the universe toward eternity
with the assurance of a stock trader,
a truck without garage or empty street.

Some say that the age of trucks shall end,
some fate-filled evening:
blaring klaxons, archangels, the four thundering
semi-trailers of the apocalypse.

Idiots. We shall give way perhaps to another supertruck one day,
next year's model, with more torque,
more rugged style, still driving like a truck
but riding like a car, while
cruise control
guides us on into the pantheon.

On the Malignancy of the Automobile

*The sun in geostationary orbit dangling from your rearview mirror
like a radiant air freshener. Its thumb compresses the vitreous fluid of
your eyeball, adjusting itself to thwart you as you shift to avoid it.
Fields of snow hard as airplane wings flame white along the road as
brown patches of the grass decline in the otherwise-cattailed ditches.
The light claws rare black patches in the fields, last year's stubble
protruding intermittently like chest hairs from Elvis's white sequined
jumpsuit.*

1.
I last hit the ditch in '77, through no fault of my own—
looked down trying to get the cap off my beer with my teeth, and
one of my brother's buddies in the front seat gave me a bump.
Couldn't see where we was going anyway, what with the lights
turned off an all:

> *Treacherous those country roads,*
> *the dark bushes, the wet ditch*
> *rubbery with tires*
> *spinning over the soft grasses and shoots of poplars,*
> *willow bushes, mosses, cattails, starling nests.*

O it hurt to accept the automobile
    was evil.

2.

I've no romantic memories to mislead me that way at least—
though I did proposition my ex-girlfriend-twice-removed
one time on the Tsawwassen highway.
She turned me down of course, her legs being
too long to get comfortable
and the road too busy.
Later she
dumped me on the same stretch of road—
set me down, gave me my
walking papers.

3.

Evil. Like if you ride it back into
childhood, in the Okanagan Valley,
summer's hot wind
winding with you along the dry hills,
car turning like a small animal on a spit,
soft suspension numbing the brain, awakening
and confusing the esophagus.

"Stop the car!" I bellow,
"I gotta THROW UP!"

But when we pull over, stop,
my stomach stops right with it,
and, recovering sufferer,
I am kicked out into the ditch:

"Well, come on, puke! You said
you hadda puke, so PUKE!"

Forced heaves exhaust the diaphragm. Amid
a sea of jeers, a crouching figure:

> *The memory throws up high and dry*
> *a crowd of nauseous things:*
> *like the muskrat I found dead on the highway*
> *one summer day and tried to skin,*
> *until its belly cavity exploded and*
> *splashed my face and clothes and absolutely everything.*
> *Good health is behovely*
> *though the road pitches and yaws unto eternity.*

4.

Brent's horse Carmen knew it—she'd
panic at roads,
squealing tires,
oil smell or fuel exhaust,
pitching a succession of riders into the ditch
when they drifted off in the saddle,

> *the hazy afternoons*
> *dreams of*
> *steamy hot Camaros with big hulking engines,*
> *stick shifts, radio knobs, and the chicks, oh yeah,*
> *chicks from Elmworth or Hinton Trail or Rio Grande,*
> *the automobile had promised us.*

5.

Watch the way a cat rides, knowing
the nature of the beast, wary, or
committing cooler-fan seppuku
on a winter morning,
warning us

of our ongoing absorption
by the wheel,
        we
had to drug my cat the one time we took him in the car—loaded
him down with Demerol, Percodan, Haldol, Phenobarbitol
and (pharmaceutical) cocaine we found in the safe of my father's
drugstore. He was kind of weird on the trip—kept sharpening his
claws on the side of my head and muttering about junk bonds,
better-fitting suits. Notice
the link between car travel and capitalism.
Urban blight. Social decay. Racism. Television.

*Your companion has inserted a cassette tape into a slot on the
dashboard. Hideous crashing and bleating sounds fill the automotive
cavern. She is seat-dancing, singing inharmoniously repeating a
melodic fragment she has managed to subsume into some pre-existing
cognitive schema. The fields are bluing in the failing light and the
road is now a gravel path trickling out across a balloon of expanding
snow.*

*Strange desires are vibrating into your mind through the steering
wheel. You want to tell lies, litter, urinate on public streets, defend
child molesters, vote Alliance, distribute toxic baby formula in Burkina
Faso, and this woman—if she could be done away with, you would be
free forever of this insufferable music.*

You glance across at her. But she is your lover!

*Reaching up to the dashboard you say quietly: "Let's play twenty
questions.*

I'll just kill this music."

Notes on the Schönfeld Airport in Berlin

1.
All time flows into airports
but the airports are never filled. It
pools in departure lounges where travellers
inhale it like opium smoke as they await their connections.
Later, updrafts of time
will carry them aloft.

2.
People are distributed equidistant in the glass container that is the
Schönfeld Airport, filling the available space like molecules in a gas. As they
bounce against surfaces within the structure they accumulate mass. I (for
example) receive a quantity of espresso in a plain clinical cup. A woman
hands me books in a beautiful cotton bag with *Berliner Zeitung* written on
it. Each interaction triggers a gentle explosion of joyfulness, which can
reach near toxic concentrations inside the terminal.

3.
Is the sky over the Schönfeld airport pure white?
Are the glass walls made of sunlight?
Or is the sky smeared
ochre printed with incomprehensible script?
The glass walls' interstellar darkness?
Or something else?
These uncertainties in no way compromise the definitive character of my
    recollection.

4.

German speakers are of course generally unaware that their language does not mark gerundive moods, as if there were no distinction between ongoing conditions and discrete events. Or perhaps they are aware that in the Schönfeld airport all conditions are ongoing, while all passages through the airport become discrete in memory, their extension fading into forgetfulness.

5.

Is there a city?

I see no broad exhausting
Kurfürstendamm, no
tangled neon,
no fur-clad prostitutes by the glass
display cases. Power
and rail lines wink
into the clear distance, the people
melting into a bright ceramic surface
which shatters as it meets the
chill vortex of time inside. Cling
to whatever flotsam
you find swirling here—
friend, father, awkward stranger displaying your name—
anyone warm.

Whale-Watching near Penhold Alberta

Inside the forest—
ripple of glistening sheet muscles the lattice
of animal trails overlaying all extremities. Silent
systalsis of the vaulted interconnecting chambers.
A vast agglomeration of separable organic
morphemes, incarnate, plunging
the inky air. 2 A.M.

Broken free from the black cord that sways
between porch and lamppost
of an ingested farmyard.

Enclosed tractor, pickup, seeder,
a rusting Oldsmobile beside the granary,
its open carburetor spilling
last season's leaves.

Congealed spermaceti of darkness accumulating in low-lying areas.

In the forest all things spiral inward, slowly, toward a centre, an arboreal
pyloric valve where darkness, attaining its absolute, transforms into its
antithesis and begins to phosphoresce.

So that like a snail's tongue the wisps of paths wind in the darkness, gradually moving closer to this point, a certain fungus on a particular decaying log. From the underside of this log it casts a soft but unnatural-looking glow over a small hollow of grass, pale Coleman lantern on a rotting roof beam. This is the reactive centre, around which porcupines drift in the gastric juices of the night, trying sleepily to hang on to the ribbed walls of hiking trails, barely noticing the glow that marks the axis of their rotation.

Moths circle too, their dorsal fins breaking the night's surface. Remora of bats. A column of invisible vapour rises from the tops of the trees, spattering the low-hanging stars. Thousands of green alveoli expand on the bronchial branches.

A hiker might spend one, two, even three days here, and leave already partly digested.

Barely aware of it.

THAT PARTICULAR MATERIALITY AND PLACENESS OR SITUATEDNESS

Site is the content, of which an architectural work might serve as the form.
-Fredric Jameson,
University of Alberta lecture, 1992

If, however, one feels that the city space of the 1980s has for all kinds of multiple and overdetermined reasons lost that particular materiality and placeness or situatedness . . . then such exegesis will come to seem misguided or irrelevant. Not wrong, necessarily, for these structures may be the remnants of an older modernist language subsumed and virtually canceled by the new one, yet persisting feebly and in a pinch decryptable by a bright and stubborn, backward-looking reader and critic.
-Fredric Jameson,
"Spatial Equivalents in the World System"

Windsor

Yellow lights in living-room windows cough and glow humbly against the unearthly glitter of the Detroit sky. Windsor is an architectural statement against the totalizing discourse of the megalopolis, a benign virus established in a tumour grown larger than its host, an alien vocabulary lost inside a dialect outstripping the mother tongue.

Obscured by the bare lightbulb of tunnels and bridges a river sniffles, seedy bar separating form from content. It must be Wednesday, for a military band wheezes in a dark drill hall, dubious arrangements of last decade's hits.

The confluence of rivulets, cold matte metal flowing into the decomposition of spring snow, snowbanks already partly sublimed into the atmosphere.

Marginal to all this a certain long weekend in Windsor many years ago— raw cauliflower as fast food, Ichiban noodles, the checkered tablecloth in Grandmother's Pizza at 3 A.M., accent lights on the street, and a long, wet shortcut through vacant lots of smooth but slumping snow.

Regina #1: Summer

In summer the bare concept of Regina is made meaningful by a hot brittle
wind blowing earthward from the sun.

What would otherwise be a mere schema stretched incarnate across the
prairie.

The urban imperialist agenda is all-encompassing but unrealizable, its
relentless piped water raising green welts on the brown landscape.
Every tree inside the city limits is artificial, embarrassed, an
uncommitted colonial reluctant to assimilate, congregating in lakeside
ghettos.

Yet the sky above rebuts definitively, eggshell radiant it nominalizes its own
act of extension, superimposing an incompatible horizon of
expectations which countenances only the landscape hidden under this
pretense of urbanity.

Paint is flaking from the debris of an abandoned convenience store.
Breaking free of the urban indoctrination a vacant lot reclaims its
identity in spear grass and foxtail.

Grasshopper wings are propaganda leaflets for the resistance, rising
everywhere from the dust, inscribed with symbols the land alone can
read.

Chicago

Hospital green of the elevated train industrial, dome lights strobing with the vehemence of each shunt.

Wheels shriek, panic, the train frame's anguish heading south from Evanston. I look out at the ruined city stretching toward the west, rotting bricks, ash-heaps sprinkled with mid-afternoon snow, a bright clothesline across the fire escape of a smashed apartment block, burnt wreckage inhabited precariously beyond the borders of civilization.

This is the site which Chicago interprets, the alluvial plain of human aspirations, the *menu peuple* scuttling amid the detritus of a mythic meritocracy, the invisible hand constructant, shifting, filtering, molding across centuries toward a moment when "class structure" is no longer a metaphor and stands revealed upon the shores of Lake Michigan.

The train plunges under the Earth. As the lights wink off in this car I see glazed faces in the next, hear the wails of unbaptized babies descending in sparks. But in the twinkling of an eye light again: our windows race along tunnel walls.

A violent shift throws several of us onto the muddy floor, grains of flour in a grimy sifter, clutching for handrails in a forest of indifferent legs.

A spark outside. Then darkness.

Regina #2: Winter

Secret oxbows of asphalt conceal hibernating Teutonic villages, long sloping eyelids flickering nocturne connotations.

The moon coasts, a slack ball valve leaking white luminescence over freshly shovelled sidewalks.

Stardust molecules bond into the fractal gaps of injured snowflakes, torn and broken against the movements of their 178,000 companions (city proper, 1996).

Snow obscures the scene.

Somewhere a Cable Regina main feeder line has cracked.

Dresden

Stones prostrated at the Schillerplatz streetcar stop. The sun.

Traveller's anomie, it's attenuated colours. Nerves filtered through words of Mitteleuropean—half-intuited archetype of a linguistic structure evolving at a speed and fluency ungraspable.

Sown through the streets are broken things, smashed windows and collapsed facades, trees growing on rubble-strewn rooftops.

The air retells its history in juxtaposed smells—the rioting life of ur-architecture, the cool darkness of linden, spruce and oak, a stratum of the Middle Ages, the Saxon Court reassembled from the dust of its ruins, coalsmoke of the DDR, concrete bus shelters, and proud curve of the *Kulturpalast*, touching in its art deco sophistication.

And for all times and places the gentle smell of the women passed on the street—pepper, moss and Kölnischwasser, the warmth of skin through the heavy air a promise of life and Lovingkindness.

Atlantis

Although in its more specific topographical aspects Atlantis resists
    revelation, most commentators agree at least on a binary nature:
    Atlantis is (a) lost, and (b) under the sea. These normally accidental
    properties elevated to the substantial.

For Scholastic philosophy therefore Atlantis is a kind of opposite of God.
    The act-of-*non*-presence (i.e. lostness which I will take as non-
    existence) functions as its essence or quiddity.

Thus existence there *does* have a predicative essence, Kant can no longer
    refute the ontological argument, and God exists—in the non-existent
    city.

Atlantis continues its shadow life at the margins of popular culture, its
    mutant superdenizen drawn in bikini-bottomed musculature, hair
    appropriately slicked back on the smudged pages of a forgotten *graphic
    novel*. In a more specialized form its inhabitants are available by mail
    order—brine shrimp with imaginary legs and crowns. For one dollar
    plus postage and handling a crystal ball of apostrophes will enter into
    the compendium of your unrealized aspirations (not exactly as shown)
    and take up residence in a shantytown on the Atlantean outskirts.

Doric columns, bones of coral made, rise out of the surplus value of submarine light, the visible manifestation of all irrevocably lost things: Okanagan summer, snows of yesteryear, the train platform in Saint-Hyacinthe where long-lost Denise kissed me once goodbye, the pre-nostalgic contemporaneity of bell-bottom jeans.

As I gaze upon its reedy acropolis, dwarfed by the circling fantail and flatfish, tirelessly vacuumed by the luminous snail, an adjacent industrial facility releases a stream of silver globules. They rise to heaven, where a roiling thundersheet filled with golden light absorbs them gratefully. Gazing across the sprawling conurbation of Atlantis I am bathed in this light, the soft purr of the oxygenator, marine shadows slithering across the carpet, the furniture, Grant and Allie's scattered toys.

Verlo, Saskatchewan

The features of Verlo's architecture
are assembled in an hierarchy of fixity:
exposed skeleton of the two grain
elevators, teeth of the hilltop black-streaked,
scattered trailers, wrecked cars, tractor tires.
The two counterweighted houses shift,
posture like bashful sumo wrestlers
behind clutched clumps of lilacs.

The road flops, slithers between them,
languidly curved umbilicus of the civic identity.

A whitewashed suburban sprawl of chickens, geese,
and
    finally:

the lone horse—CN Tower trembling
over the elaborate landscape,
stark in the blue evening shadows, the pulsing
airplane-warning lights of its forelock.

The contextualization of metropolitan Verlo's
urban architecture is gratifyingly absolute—
hayrows following and
accentuating the undulating land,
encircling hilltops and boulders.
The moon at their peak, a
perfect hemisphere
above the red clay lakeshore,
Verlo [Spanish, = to see it], dissolving at several speeds at once
fades into a perfect genius loci—
two yellow eyes with kitchen tables, wall clocks,
dusty faces and International Harvester ball-caps.
From the heart of the metropole
a blue 1964 Bel Air winds its way up the uneven road,
stares briefly into your headlights
and continues on its way.

The Gingerbread House (after Humperdinck)

First is the problem of distinguishing site from structure
since neither Forest nor House exist, mere
extrapolations of post-Wagnerian longings.
The Holy Wood has been constructed
out of the reified boundary of
phenomenal experience turned to sound,
valleys and walls of it.

There are features aporic:
the warm chords of summer against snow
heavy on the spruce boughs, or the
white icing beside the hearth-warm carpet of soft
needles, the glistening icicles over a meadow
of summer strawberries,
and, as the sun sets Caspar Friedrich
behind a painted knoll, the Sandman
tiptoes up in his cone-shaped hat
and fourteen angels fold sheltering wings
over Gretel's sleeping limbs.

The forest is a swell of nocturnal sound even in the daytime—
the mossy undergrowth of horns
and cuckoo call of flute and oboe. Beyond
Hänsel's awareness we hear the reedy machinations of the fox
and the dark squirrels of the violas. Gretel,
nestled in the oak
is untroubled by the white hart and
unicorn hidden behind the foliage out of sight.

Children clamour after the enchanted forest
(off Highway One near Revelstoke for example), they crave
the stony paths arrayed in spiral toward the centrepiece,
the gingerbread house,
marzipan doors framed
with jujube emeralds and cinnamon hearts, opening
on the gobble witch, her sonic maw.

Let the flavour dissolve in your mouth,
sweet precipitate of the acoustic forest,
its Christmas colours all
bundled up in *Fachwerkbau* and the laughing fence
of gingerbread children now restored.

STATIONS OF THE HIGHWAY

Stations of the Highway with Undiagnosed Pneumonia as Summer Heats Up

Aluminum ribs panting for departure
while at the machine's nucleus a
sagging, phlegm-oozing lung lies
                              prostrate for assessment.
A hot bacteria fist is wrapped around a fat
theopathic organ,
squeezing the
neurotransmissionary juices
     out to sizzle on the pavement.

>   . . . *I got fever and became delirious and unconscious*. . .
>
>   (On the Road)

     Fever haloes the
          instrument panel, windshield reflections, traffic lights—

a rip in bronchi
elongates to fill the whole compartment,
lifts me to
          ignition. . .

1. Regina Mohawk

Reading:

Regina falls away,
my ass hurtling,
centimetres from the asphalt
    caged corpuscle in aluminum overwrap
    bound for the
    throbbing Jarvik model-2000 artificial
        heart of southern Ontario.

Exhortation:

Consider the verdant glade of land—
the vegetable garden of earth
    and because the world
    because the world is
    because the world is full of
        cold pools, old fools,
            dark pods, hot rods.
              Poets.
    Do not scruple to ride.

Prayer:

Not to traverse,
    transnutate, transnavigate this road,
but to inhabit, to haunt it,
    draw close around me
        the grey mantle of its length,

to furnish my indwelling
    with tires and chrome lamps
        cough candies lined up on the coin tray,

to apprehend in the far-off eucalyptus haze
day after weary day away,
Ontario towns peripatetic toward sunrise, their
        wanderings in maple groves by the roadsides
          and the still,
                intellectual lakes.

2. Balgonie Tempo

Reading:

The road in phases like the moon
waning in the steam of afternoon

floats in the blue liquid air, half-
submerged, fissured features miraged upon it.

Rinds of tar peel and contract as they
bleed from an asphalt terminator line, and

ruins of a Roman watchtower glower
from barleyfield bed of Glacial Lake Regina.

Mounting the aspen lands, kettle lakes hiss and steam
latex pigment pots for the mixing of sky and reeds.

My transit capsule subsumes all these sounds into
roar of wind, drowning
the *vox populis* (species: *tremuloïdes*),
the taller grasses shuffling
around their algae-spackled cauldrons.

Exhortation:

Consider the occupation
of this space, the highway, aspire this a habitat—
draw around yourself
this asphalt cloak, and become habituated
to the inhabitation of motion, all the reifying capacities
of late consumer capitalism
brought to bear on this equation,
the relation of habit to monk, of

space to trajectory, occupation
of pure moment, momentum, its assimilation
into the sedentary activity of habitation,
accumulation inside this one line, building
toward plenitude in its one dimension.

𝔓𝔯𝔞𝔶𝔢𝔯:

To narrow, narrow within as day recedes,
while the road Turneresquely turns
  flows out onto the ground
    of groundsel and yarrow,
     grama and spear grass of the still plane.

To be the road, the fever, that oncoming rise
a wave
  propagated along the grasses
    rippling the foxtail, the coneflowers, the fescue.
The primordial landscape revived by the sunlight
  and the fever which echoes it.

My road is the sickbed of saints, their slow decline
through infection,
to the soft pool of the universe, horizon
yearning to close, to plunge with them,
Ignatius, Francis, Theresa, into the fevered depths,
medium of their
several conversions.

> *I saw his huge face over the plains with the mad, bony purpose and the*
> *gleaming eyes; I saw his winds; I saw his old jalopy chariot with*
> *thousands of sparking flames shooting out from it. . .*   (On the Road)

3. Moosomin Fas Gas

Reading:

Not much endless prairie here. Surmounting
the strand lines of glacial Lake Regina
the land is disoriented, dizzy,
overcome with rubble. Kettles "an
ubiquitous and attractive feature." Aspen
wander the landscape in
scraggly gangs, gathering by kettleside to
murmur and plot against nature.

Though some of these are sacred groves.

Exhortation:

Consider that although the land along what we call Highway One is almost
entirely "alienated for agriculture," the ditches still evoke occasionally their
primordial state; blue grama and spear grass vying for dominance;
sagebrush gleaming like unnatural lips in a velvet painting.

Consider how the prairie surrounds but does not absorb, the road
cone-shaped as I look down into it, the sinister
hooded eyes of oncoming vehicles.
The road extending eastward without
vanishing point,
asymptote of continuity,
comet's open parabola, alembic of the
visual dimension.

And consider the afternoon's shifting hips under a gauze dress of light,
clutter of butterflies, milkweed stalks
smeared on the shoulder, leaking
into my eyes, and off
into the
    imagined roll
        of imagined uplands.

Prayer:

O to sleep, that gluey pressure on my tongue
spelling instructions in the decay of
systoles, rhythm to arrhythm.

Tires. Tired. Tirade. Radials.
Radiating from their rotation, Secanol hubcaps
go-go spiral behind sunflower drumthrob.

Longing is a line pulled through my skin
drawing me toward dashboard,

                      pavement,
      annihilation
like the
deer leaping into annihilation, that
yellow roadsign, deer,
    desperately panting for streams, running
        streams of consciousness,
                    unconsciousness. . .

4. Falcon Beach Shell

Reading:

The secret bedroom of cars
enclosed in the green of roadside poplars.
Lined along the woodline, lined
with sleep, across from the washroom cabin.
Children and toothbrushes march there
in their flannel pyjamas
from a blank-eyed camper. A 1967
Plymouth Mastodon dozing, windows veiled
with lace curtains. Other cars, cowled
like monks asleep at compline,
sag. They loll in the
darkness like snoozing
manatees, rare headlights
from the highway tracing
fingers of shadow across their backs, a
caress of light outstretched through the trees.

At dawn all have disappeared. A sign proclaims:
"Rest area closed 11:00 P.M. to 9:00 A.M."

Exhortation:

Consider the hollow in the wood,
in the median, a coat pocket
where a pet dormouse might curl asleep,
peeking out for snuffling
or for treats.

Night in the hollow however
excruciating, the choice between
stagnant air in a sealed vehicle or

car windows open to the barrage of mosquitoes
already deployed on the windshield.

The hollow first signalled
by the alienation of the oncoming lane,
the highway a vector abruptly rendered
unidirectional as time.

Consider time, into sleep, partial sleep.
The near border of Ontario tonight.

Prayer:

All I ask of this road, this
land, this ride, is that it give way forever
to a
state-of-the-art recliner rocker
on a porch by a door.
And sitting in it there to sip,
Ciproxin or some cheaper but
equally effective antibiotic
through a straw,
and to sleep upright,
horking up now and again a
good green phlegmball
into the brass cuspidor beside me.

> *I looked out of the dark swirl of my mind and I knew I was on a bed
> eight thousand feet above sea level, on the roof of the world, and I knew
> that I had lived a whole life and many others in the poor atomistic husk
> of my flesh, and I had all the dreams. . .*   (On the Road)

5. Thunder Bay Beaver

Reading:

Advancing through the rock forest
the ditches fill dangerously with
deer made of shadow, their interlocking
shapes composing ideographic characters impossible
to read in this shitty light.

The illuminated manuscript runs, the running deer—
ink leaking slowly into the
bottom edge of sky.

Peripherally I detect their flashbulb eyes
along the narrowing promontory of pavement that
thrusts up into the heart of the lake. This is
the walk-in closet of nocturnal highway,
Ignace to Thunder Bay a narrow
passage weakly defined by these cheap
standard-equipment GM headlights.

Exhortation:

Consider Thunder Bay enclosed in its picket fence,
the first layer of surrounding forest now
                petrified by the night so that,
joining the old stone of the Precambrian shield,
phylogeny recapitulates *orogeny*.
Thunder Bay a cottage surrounded
by a dark wood where
dark creatures: grey badgers,
    least weasels, arrange themselves
in allegorical tableaux behind black
butterflies on wings borrowed from fruit bats,
fluttering through
ancient deadfall, between the
crisscross latticed
    eyebeams of the squirrels.

And consider how Kakabeka Falls by the
roadside leading into Thunder Bay—
the tusks of grey sills towering at sunset
    above the highway, shell
after shell of pitted,
    acne-scarred cliff marking its tormented
oro-adolescence, under a cornice of
    receding soil—crumbles.

𝔓𝔯𝔞𝔶𝔢𝔯:

To follow that access road,
the blue jellyfish evening-gown roadsign where Kakabeka Falls—
    opening to the revelation of
    wheels
        of spray
        rolling
                beneath the Earth
                through claws of rumpled rock,
                Sphinx rampant—riddles
                the falls with refuse
                of bygone kills:
                roar of water through the rock,
                      severed jawbone of rock

loud as lumber trucks on that plunging riverbed rolling
    granite windshield wipers scraping hard slate
        overcome with the height and
            volume of the river's
                pounding—there to be seen,
                    or so I imagine
                behind the highway's cool green sign.

*Committed to the idea that beauty and power production can co-exist
Ontario Hydro entered into an agreement in 1962 guaranteeing much
higher minimum flows over the falls during tourist season: fixed
minimum flows during daylight hours June 1 to September 30: 300
cubic feet/second on weekends and holidays and 150 cubic feet/second
on weekdays.*   (Ontario Hydro)

6. Marathon G&A Lucky Star

Reading:

Filling-station pumps are Wagnerian
in their square-helmeted Teutonic postures,
Ontario banners flying in the
lavender-water version of *Wille zur Macht*.

Night after unbearable night I see them posturing
against a shabbily illumined stage cluttered
with sets and props selected from
The Golden Bough—rites
of the road Trans-Canadian.

High here on the shore of Lake Superior I reach
Marathon, the gas pumps thrusting their cultural roots
deep into the Precambrian rock,
gorging themselves on the thickening E-flat triads,
exalted, immobile, often
heartbreakingly lyrical as they resonate
across the Shield's many amphitheatres.

Exhortation:

Veronica—so her name tag proclaims—
considers me,
my croaked "fill-er-up," out-of-province plates, ruin of
books-on-cassette, used bottles and packaging
littering my compartment.

Considers my swollen throat ground to rock flour
by the action of Precambrian pneumococcus.

I close my eyes to consider the slow rotation
of the observer homunculus detaching
from its positional slots—wipe,

                 squeak,

                         wipe.

Each extended blink leaves time
to undermine
my confidence in a fixed horizon,
chamois cloths
waving like blue kelp
under my flagging eyelids.
Veronica considers.
Time to pay.
Taps at the window.

𝔓rayer:

To be saved from this road, syringe filled with
barely necrotized contagions,
tangling in the blue confusion
of my veins.

From this road, the grey flannel pyjama of it,
where the steam of each breath reveals
windshield wiping streaks
superimposed on my way.

7. Sault Ste. Marie Husky with Truck Stop

Reading:

Morning is not a sickness but the exposed fundament of human ontology.

Fingers tremble on the steering wheel as
dashboard monitors register
dangerous insufficiencies of

glucose
caffeine
T-cells
serotonin
dopamine
enkephalin
DNA . . . love.

This cat's not home and the mice aren't just playing around anymore.

Purple warning lights aswarm with *muscae volitantes* block
orientation as dawning consciousness clears to reveal:
plastic menus, checkered tablecloth
and a view of the highway
aglow with possibilities.

Exhortation:

Consider this intersection
of the alimentary canal and Trans-Canada Highway,
its many stations, geographical anomalies,
backwaters, emulsifiers, astringents, corrosive agents.

Consider my Last Supper, not long before departure,
a conversation in which everyone participates equally, a
community actively existing, a

village like Echo Bay, looking inward,
gastronomically enraptured, while a ring of highway
is built around them, access ramp
extrapolated from every habitation
however humble.

Consider then how this communion establishes the
absences which accompany you on your journey, a
summer evening on the feast of Bartholomew,
assembled in your kitchen, after sunset, plates
of corn chowder, "Farewell
to Nova Scotia" sung in Saskatchewan and the bubbles
of Lovingkindness dissolving out of your blood in
tiny delicious pops.

Prayer:

Bless us O Lord and after supper was ended
(many suppers past)
there were these plates
these stacks of plates and cups and casserole
dishes eggplant
ground in the carpet and
milk in ginger, a roux in saucepan,
wineglasses on the clock the
fridge the open cupboard the magazine rack the
front porch
back porch
underbed,
serving spoons beside the recliner and
in the shadows which then closed around
the small

      squat

      very empty house.

8. Iron Bridge Nugget

The highway melts
into a midsummer
spring of afternoon, a torrent sluicing down
the inflamed capillary of road coursing
through the deteriorating tissues of Iron Bridge Ontario,
                    its gravelled roadside.

And there is a woman walking on the roadside.

Coming out of the convenience store I see girls lounging on the hoods of
    cars parked in the parking lot of the adjacent school. They lean
    forward and back as they pass cigarettes.

I notice the woman I drove past on the road, her white T-shirt and hiking
    boots, standing behind the cars on the grass, listening, a quality of
    listening which seems to focus the attention of the others more sharply
    on each other.

She is now barefoot and holds a pet rodent between nearly prehensile toes,
    a rat perhaps, caressing its long tail with her other foot. I wonder how
    she can do this without falling over and decide to cross the parking lot
    to see more closely but before I do the group suddenly disperses,
    driving away in their cars.

The barefoot woman is halfway across the schoolyard before I locate her
    with an acute and unexpected sense of loss, her shoulder blades
    shifting visibly under her T-shirt, her wings barely moving as they hold
    her aloft.

Exhortation:

Consider the town of Iron Bridge, east of the Soo, the
ditches, the afternoon sun bleaching the gravel.

Consider the metaphor of dust, the handprint of mustardseed, thin
muscles of a girl in leotards attempting cartwheels.

Iron Bridge arranged in stations, locks of land with
swing sets, tree houses, automobile parts. Here and there
a dollhouse or teepee, proprietor posed beside, with
wire-haired terrier or dachshund.

There is *Destruktion* along the main road, propositions
annihilating against anti-propositions along the streets,

and her longish hair as she vanishes through the chain-link,
woven together into a robe for the disrespect
of shoulders—casting of lots to follow
in an upcoming parking lot later.

Prayer:

All I ever wanted was,
I wanted always and forever.
All I wanted ever was,
I wanted all of this forever
because
all I ever wanted was
　　　　to weep with you
　　　　　　　women of Jerusalem.

9. Thornbury Esso

Reading:

The night intersects the rain
at the Owen Sound interchange,
drenched dark on the black
Orangeville road undetectable
slick charcoal road by the hedgerows,
skidding on the precarious seal fur of slope,
toward the wet accumulation of distant lights

and there the sign for Thornbury, where
Abraxas, Defender of the Galaxy lowbudge Can-flick was
shot on location and with gratitude
to the people and café
and tenebrous woods of wet snow
through my apartment VCR,
the long shadows of poplar
and pine trees and
thrashing through the driven dark of Thornbury—

The unknown strangers arriving in the Hometown Café of Thornbury the
 locals gathered round their coffee suspicious of slick-suited interlopers
 but little imagining

the cosmic crisis as Abraxas finds the boy the chosen one in the house by
 the river's dark water under the stone bridge the snowy banks and
 brave single mother (widowed) her unspoken affiliation with handsome
 town sheriff.

Their reception of wounded and socially awkward interstellar visitor brave
   (and beloved?) sheriff opposing twelve-gauge to interstellar plasma
   dematerialization beams hand-held particle lasers of sinister strangers
   surrounding the home

so that wounded Abraxas must needs lure them while breaking through the
   ice crust on featureless no-place-to-hide fields

and in direct confrontation saving child and galaxy from annihilation
   Götterdämmerung and credits thank you especially people of
   Thornbury Ontario especially.

Exhortation:

Consider these trucks outlined in swaths of sequins
shrinking below me, the golden highway light, my
car shunting on its rails, ascending.

Consider the festive glow
of this lantern procession,
life seeping from a contingent of arthropod party guests
into the world beyond,
their fur, leather, and yellow jackets draped
ever-so-casually across speeding windshield wipers and
grille
   of interlocking crosses.

Prayer:

To be lifted
in an aerial car, a car aerial
broadcast across the night.

In the racked soil of my silted tongue, to
feel the passage
of Sauble Beach passing, the
summer winds whipping flags, tire tracks in the sand.

Somewhere the tectonic plates of my skull
have collided, over the works of days and ears,
while the dark streams of this rain wash crosses
across my swollen body, nasal and cardiac septum
pierced to flow together, southward
toward Lake Ontario.

> . . . *the third day I began having a terrible series of waking nightmares,
> and they were so absolutely horrible and grisly and green that I just lay
> there doubled up with my hands around my knees, saying, "Oh, oh, oh,
> ah, oh. . ."*   (On the Road)

10. Dundas Ultramar

Reading:

The road winds down
toward leafy Dundas, where the escarpment
ridge of leaf, rock wall,
curls round the lake. Three
days from the prairie.

Warm rain on
slick streets and a sky
fortress of phosphorescent powders.
Columns of lit rain posture
like incandescent bodybuilders
above the dripping streetlamps.

Several things I wondered in the slick
     pre-dawn parking lot, whether
     the porch light really welcomed, and if so
     whom, with such coldness, in the
     extravagant night, the water running
     by the curbside and fanning out over the street,
whether, climbing the steps, the fixity
     of this dwelling would suffice
     to quell the ongoing motion—

of the lines, stretched, diverging
lines, of the igneous mind and unseen
grassland, the aspen and batholiths run
through beaches of hematite, the blind
conifers of a land and driving,

    forever driving,

        rain.

Exhortation:

Consider yourself as you
draw close around you this dark mantle
of dwelling, lined with sandstone, the breathless
oblivion of space,

draw it closely around you, the cloak of the house,
the distant lapping lake,
this fixity

    integral.

  Consider yourself well in.

Prayer:

Bless the soft

    rain patterned

  baroque

    on the porch steps

drops breaking

  on my

    rain hat.

Bless the wet brick, blank

  italic, the cold

    globe of welcome light.

A sign says:

"Shoes in the closet please." The click
    of deadbolt. The hamster
        snuffles, runs again its lonely wheel
            while home, upstairs, is sleeping and
                tomorrow, perhaps,
                    notice.
                          Diagnosis.

*The whole neighbourhood was concerned. They came in and found me
lying on the bed with my arms stretched out forever. . .*
                                    (On the Road)

GUEST HOMILISTS

Fr. Leonardo Boff O.F.M. Constructs a
Phenomenology of Cognition

*"I am lying right now," says Captain James T. Kirk staring smugly into the
eyes of the hapless android before him. The android stiffens. Smoke pours
from its ears. Lies.*

You can't hide yer lyin' eyes.

(I am lying right now, too. That is:
saying things I don't know how to say,
saying them anyway. Like this.)

Mirror mirror
on the wall. You're
lying. Lying lying lying lying.

The face in the mirror. The head
    in the mirror
glanced at me furtively,
    dishonestly.

The face in the mirror under the elevator
    (in the Eaton Centre)
across from the pink neon sign
glanced at me
    (and a girl smiled to a friend
    as they passed by
    reminding me of a girl I must have known who
    can smile like this girl
    but does not smile
    like this girl)
furtively. A lie.

And yes! I confess it was a lie
when I told Floyd Halcourt I had
felt up this girl named Sandra on the beach
near Kelowna. And that she was
better-looking than Jacquie Hogg
and had bigger tits too.

And that I liked Labatt's Blue
better than Molson Canadian,
smoked Player's filters,
or won twenty-four free games
on the pinball machine at Sam's Café.

Lies. Damned lies.

I told Father Soo I didn't believe in God.
He didn't believe me. "Liar." he said.
　　　"You're lying. Pseudo-atheist. Fake." Much as
Jesus had called down to me from the cross
on day fourteen of the Spiritual Exercises of St. Ignatius,
fixing me with bloodshot eyes. "Charlatan.
You lie.
You were never one of mine,"
he in his agony, his charred arms
and sharp red teeth.

The checkout girl stares disapprovingly across the stack of pornographic movies I am renting. "And you a man o' the cloth!" she thinks.

The face in the mirror across the table
    in Friendly's Bar is speaking.
"What do you think is the best form of contraception?"
    asks Monica brightly. She dips a nacho
in green guacamole.

I am sitting next to a fire by the Redwillow River. The sun is too low in the sky to give much warmth, but fills the column of smoke from our fire with a brightness that makes it stand out eerily against the green sky. Unbeknownst to us, Kevin and I will be branding cattle tomorrow for the first and only time in our lives.

The future bellowing in the brown sun. Drool trails and sun beams.
    Fire and electric prods, broken hockey sticks, blood, shit and
    terror.

"Do you beat off much?" asks Kevin.
"Not really, estimated companion," I reply.
"The truth is, I have never experienced
self-induced ejaculation. I suspect I am defective;
perhaps I shall consult my physician."

I adjust my clothes. Check
for protruding nasal hairs.
Reflections are deceptive:
my movements reflect back more quickly
    than I perform them:

*Cynthia and I first spent the night together when the brown lawn was
already visible and covered with sticky gauze. The town smelled of damp
rot; a tire beside the highway stood on a pedestal of snow; ice cracked under
mats of leaves.*

So very important.

*But already it was over while crews were still putting flowerpots in public
boulevards. Tourist season had yet to begin. A passage of six arguments.
Three lunar cycles. Fifteen laundry loads.*

Time is not meaning. Time is a lie.
Only in gerunds lies the truth.

The face in the mirror in the hollow place
    under the refrigerator. Humming.
    Beware of refrigerators bearing gifts.
A yellow-eyed cat spits down from the holy rood:
"You were never one of mine." Hiss.

"How do you know when a stockbroker's lying?"

God, on the other hand, is incapable of deceit. Lacks imagination.

"Well I wouldn't call myself a compulsive masturbator."
"Twice a week."
"Twice a day."
"In the bathroom."
"Powder my nose."
"Freshen up."
"A below-average student."
"Father, I . . . I . . . went to Sherbrooke,
Trois-Rivières, Abitibi and other places."
"An untruth"
"I know."
"I don't know."

"You're a fake," says Captain James L. Shaddai, staring smugly into the face of the hapless mendicant before him. The cleric's eyes implode like a television tube 1958 RCA Victor. Lips writhe like a sidewalk earthworm.

Hide the you you've got inside.

Walks with Humane Society's David Suzuki Jones
"Zuki" b.2000–d.2001

1.
Zuki in his warm sweater and Halti collar on
mornings when it was unbearably cold.

Except that we bore it.

2.
So many connections
between snow and
other snow,
scooped smoothly into passageways
like cream cheese brushed
one whiteness degree whiter with Petrodex
for dogs (delicious!). The wind that
wound along the slots of the paths.

I realized then as I now
realize, that there was brown
earth always under the snow.

And I felt a degree of love
for the small streams
that started up one day, though
none for the snowbanks that turned
brown and grey,
layered themselves away,
like dirty plates.

Because snow is a trick.
Like the clouds from a plane

sun on their backs, their spouting
silver muzzles and fields of Zukiteeth,
cave after catacomb that calls through the portholes:

Embrace me, my sweet embraceable you.

Though it's unfair to criticize I suppose—
as all is mortal under the sun.
Just as temporary really are the snow
caves over sewer grates or
grottoes and cathedrals of limestone beneath the Earth.

Yet faced with the *real caves* I have to tell myself, "real
these caves are real" knowing
they'll disappear too someday, they're
only limestone after all.

3.
"Pulling? Leash-pulling? No, we don't have any
pulling dogs here. We walk *together*,
because. . . now what is this?"
So I stopped to observe another snowbank
melting. "Hmm. Now to your
alien intelligence,
tracing anomalies in the formula of air,
trajectories of winds passing
at superhuman frequencies, the signature of
feet, feces and scentmarks, passage
and intention of bird, disposition of
dormant mycillium, first stirrings of
insect embryos in the thawing soil, these
shapes are, or are they not,
mundane?"

Evenso affection stirred in me
for this bright snowbank,
its wild topography, and he?

4.
Pulling toward the approaching Golden Retriever on the path
Pulling toward the jackrabbit on the ball diamond
Pulling toward the plastic bag blowing by the artificial waterfall
Pulling toward the magpie trashtalking from a tree
Pulling toward the Crazy Carpet in the ice bowl
Pulling toward Clint and Jules coming up the street
Pulling toward Cinder in the schoolyard
Pulling toward a driveway full of mist after midnight,
laundry mist reluctant to depart,
circling between a house and hedge,
in the partial light of the neon house number
and the streetlamp blocked by a hawthorn, which Zuki
analyzed and knew:
whose laundry it was,
who had worn what, or lent to guests,
what brand of detergent and fabric softener they'd used
whether they'd sweated profusely or used antiperspirant,
what they had eaten that week,
whether they were in love
and with whom? Each other or
parties outside the household?

*These dogs must be taught not to pull when they are puppies, for
as adults they are immensely strong.*

6.
Envoi: Prince of the world
over all dogs sovereign—
the commodity of.
"I lay in sweet flowers." Within.

Elms although the neighbours.
Aluminum although the chimneys.
Terriers of spring
on the cold earth divining.

Elvis Foretells his Resurrection from the Dead in a Scene from *GI Blues* in Which a Record Player Breaks Down and He Saves the Puppet Show with His Singing and Dancing

And I shall write my law on their hearts.
    (Elvis is not dead.)
And the sun of justice shall return on high.
    (He lives.)

    And this is just like him—
    that face of his in the movies like wax fruit—

(I heard of a vulgar infidel who debunked the resurrection with doggerel
    about the myth of Elvis, a *reductio ad Elvis* cynicism. Wipe that snicker
    off your face, lecteur.)

No! what I am trying to get at is
is, well (and all manner of thing shall be well) is this:
There is a moment. The moment. When things
change. Or have been changed. A moment with bells.
When every (single) (little) head [shall] bow. Knees shall bend,
yea even an angel shall bend the knee
though they don't have any.

You know, street numbers and how they go on
through leafy suburbs bell-jarred into tranquility
until they are a new street with a new name and
when they became this new thing and
although Parmenides thought change was impossible
how did it get there then and
how did it get to be spring I ask you. Which it
was and then

wasn't and fools said in their heart it
wasn't so and so they just
rushed in.

A night and Jupiter's four moons
telescopian over a cabin in the Bruce Peninsula.
The shivering porch-dark and that movie
sniggering in the vox populi,
and the flat rocks stretching
to the bushes, black water
peeking over the rock-lip at the blue light window.
Ice and the smoke rising smudged on the stars.
All hidden.
These things around us are confused yes
no actually the moment the moment
is transplanted. Jupiterian
ice night a night
haunted all Io and Ganymede. But the moments are connected.
Absolutely connected.

These are invisible dividers. Tropics of
imperceptible seasons, you crossed them—
observe the changed
climate, the strange bird sounds
ferns and exotic fungi. And smiles now
different now, beyond this or other antipode—
and further. A new and
unreachable before. Not even desired.
Could you have ever understood it?
Could you even now?

> *Elvis' head now swaying like an inflating dirigible, his latex cheeks*
> *and eyebrows drooping across the puppet stage. A slouching vocal*

movement posed in your own proximity. Do you remember? He sings
"Sei mir gut, sei mir gut," in flawless German. "Cause I don't have a
wooden heart."

A voice that slides and tunnels through the
dust of your hyper-education, your cynicism,
worms into the wood of the cross. Elvis is it? Elvis's Easter?
The song of (all you) angels around God's throne. I could hardly
blame people (the people) for their attachments
their faults, for this *felix culpa*, yet
if only there weren't so many *infelix culpas* to go with it.

Karl Rahner called this *Ausschau*, the being-on-the-lookout for something
significant-for-salvation (translations my own). The orientation
absolute.

> *Dust of roof snow the wide undulations*
> *of temperature graphable in the inefficiencies*
> *of a leaking wood stove*
> *this very-late-at-nightness*
> *accumulating underneath our eyelids. Halos form*
> *around the cheekbones of our hero. Without*
> *of course impairing the functioning of the*
> *two-track monophonic VCR playing a rented copy of*
> GI Blues. *But Brad has stopped suggesting*
> *we turn it off.*

And Elvis. Elvis Orpheus in the slow decay of their imperceptible accompanist. Elvis and a puppet dancing, jumpy as a puppet on a string. Not that he is any different now, the soft porcelain of his reconstituted sneer-smile collapsing in a rain of golden records. Elvis the holdup man of our fleshly hearts, condom nylon-stockinged over his smooth face in that rain of golden records, the topknot reservoir and tympanic surface stretched across his lips soothing. A hidden life. The near-sneer meaning. But not a sneer.

Transfiguration. Transitions. Invisible dividers.
And you have crossed them? Perhaps,

because it was then that you realized he had
won you over and that you would bathe in steel!
(Or is that "beg and steal"?)
but death could never keep him from you.

The VCR plays on into the consecration of his gyrations. You are the wooden puppet with whom he dances, Pinocchio, bobbing and kissing the giant smiling face that will now hang suspended above your nighttime vigils. Remember this moment, your path.

Credits roll. The small screen transcended is now behind us. He will be with us, beyond time, beyond the GI blue window. Sleeping bags spread in the dark corners of the cabin, stars in the window.

Embers glow in the wood stove.

Peg, Max, Gertrude Stein and I Watching
Daytime Drama

Lego wood blocks,
bears,
books,
all across the floor. This is
the
TV. Then.

"This is today's today which is a very belled saxophone to a width of
Tuesdays. A bag of replies plying over and over a pith with the most
untoward of green please dust icicles there many Roman probosci. Take off
your helmet and I'll kiss your kiss your kiss your many sparkling bottle
water glass. Chinese appendages. Without collaboration."

You are not paying attention
        to the green-on-green screen
        pictures. Rather the room. The concept of
reillumination, since the outside sky can be quite clearly seen above a
        horizon of corrugated metal around the window wells.
On the inside is.
And the silence composed of outside. Dripping faucet a vacuum cleaner of
        passing cars the squeegee intermittent of backyard birds.
Overlay of.

"Household appliances.
Mixmasteration.
Aeration. Are you a watercress smile?
All the goats carpeting. Pretty things.
Bottlegreen got to bream.
Bottlegreen whether."

Imagine the air in the room settling
itself into the irregular shape of scattered clothing and
embracing the half-eaten banana. A hint of pine tar
and increased humidity toward the bathroom hallway
indicate a recent shower even as the smells diffuse
into the living room. Toward the kitchen three white globes of light
reflect off streaks of spilled alphabet soup on a highchair.

Perhaps the banana is nearer three-quarters eaten.

The proportions of silence change. A wind has picked up
outside. The sleeping baby in the next room is dreaming
of the alphabet soup, spelling words he wouldn't recognize
even if you read them. The TV.

*Every day that goes by. The last evening. Penelope stands against the green
heath, tears streaming from her large sincere deep blue eyes set wide apart
streaming across her full red pouting quivering lips she is thinking of the
man who murdered her grandfather ruined her brother defiled her mother
poisoned her goldfish and is about to become her husband. The television
bubbling strands of mop head across the antique hardwood floors of her
aristocratic Victorian Chippendale Edwardian mansion. But Shane
Umbilicus had a charm few women could resist, his long muscular torso
rippling oh-so-thinly concealed beneath his tailored tweed English Armani
coat hinting at the raw crunchy masculine power like his deep baritone chin
cleft jutting cobalt eyes his graceful yet assured yet imposing movements his
tan blond and muscular penis which could single-handedly stimulate any
woman into uncontrollable cascades of violent orgasms, even after a heavy
meal. Great rippling slabs of beef CAKE.*

Gertrude interrupts quoting herself as she sometimes does
(from *Tender Buttons*): "CAKE."
They kept to the way because the way one.
The wave of green baize by. The furze
until the sky. The baize is furze and the furze prefers
to be baste. The water lip is last.
We would have you like them. Have you
like two. Two to be the sky.
Two to be dry. Two
to be alive. Two to be alive and
to shy. This is why.
That is what one is. With. If
it were cake.
As if it were dry.

UNPRODUCTIVE CAPITAL

The Surplus Value of the Open Road

The Cities of the Plain extremely, and their circulatory system, the
Union Station of Eros and the same, sad,
skein of *Passagenwerk* over every province,
the way you can see the hollow insides of the Earth
through the black ice on the highway,
a window on the secret world inside—Agharta, where
Hitler and Edmund Halley enjoy a comfortable retirement—
or the high roads, the high high roads so
    vastly above the other roads
        and the churning river—
the decrepit gravel road encirling Uranus,
grass between the wheel ruts and clunk
of your tires as you cross into the richer inlying planets.

You can read it like a book the scrawl of
roadways conjoining the towns and asteroids,
curving along the iron safety-rails of Saturn's
many-laned ringroad, a forgotten book
accumulating library fines vertiginously
in a city you'd forgotten you'd ever lived in.

Loss at the Black Forest Inn

No more shall I, since I am driven hence,
Devote to thee, my grains of frankincense
                                        -Robert Herrick

Scene 1: *The Apophatic Forest*
This Black Forest is wearing black leather pants and knows
three chords.

It is not the leafy Ilsenstein with sun-dappled pathways,
underbrush containing Easter bunnies
crouching shyly to be petted. There are no
clearings furnished with deck chairs of warm rock,
no grassy meadows ringed with bluebells and hollyhocks.
Bumblebees are not sun-drunk in their
loose-fitting sweaters and they *would*
dream of stinging. The wild rose does not
lower her eyelashes above a
checkerboard of strawberries, tiny
neon lanterns nodding *Yes!*
Pick me, pick me! There are no
holly trees alive with
larks and hummingbirds, no oaks
under whose gnarled gaze
a butterfly (*Nymphalis carmen*)
alights in your hair.

Mist did not appear, a silver haze among
the glitter of poplars, with the advent of evening,
and eyes do not flicker amid dark branches,
the strange blink polyphemic of
moth wings, lynx,
and shadow voles.

All forests are black in the dark
but the Ontario forest, they've eaten its heart
and the blackness of absence has hardened

into a motor hotel with dollhouse diorama—castle, inn,
Black Knight in armour under a
plywood sign in black paint,

a garage band of creative anachronisms, a
Traynor YBM-3 amp and Bloc 80B for the bass,
frayed extension cord in the tall grass.

At night and approached from the north the sign looms
from the blear like a T-shirt, *Black Forest Tour 2001:*

Thunder Bay Kennebec Iron Bridge Sault Ste. Marie
but in fact the inn has never moved, it's you, unwilling roadie—

reverb in the guitar as a few hundred years go by,
cheapest accommodation on the Trans-Canada

in the Forest of the Night. Confusing. Which
is why I lock my keys in the car.

Scene 2: *Dramatic Irony Variation*
Now included in the diorama under the black sign and behind
the screen door wrenched.
The bathroom light inclined to greenness.
Beds concave, presumed clean until proven otherwise.

Water ropey and the bathroom floor heaved in the impecunious light.
Keys on the chipped coffee table, ashtray approximately
empty. Chill on the mustard-coloured shadows.

Examining the room I have not yet learned I am
outside the windshield sealed, the dashboard casting
a shadow across the seats, alienated from
keys, toothbrush,
        wallet, pyjamas.

Scene 3: *The Exclusionary Proscenium*
Few terrestrial environments can rival the hermeticism of the *car with keys
locked inside it*, the closest analogue being the *dead language papyrus*, into
which the hapless researcher peers, sometimes frantically, already generally
aware of pyjamas, toothbrush, wallet and keys locked somewhere inside yet
able to perceive only meaningless forms—sunflower-seed-hull hills? Pop
bottles? Speculations slide off the aerodynamic surfaces of the windows, the
dead interior. Life inside a language just *too familiar* until the moment they
changed the locks, cancelled your health coverage, moved the call centre to
Dar es Salaam. That book on the driver's seat appears to be *The
Monadology*, though you hadn't brought it.

Scene 4: *Panorama*

The howl of the trucks is rarer now.
    A shy dog patrols along the row.

The lights are green on the polyester blanket.
Ghosts cup their hands to peer inside.
They ripple across the drapes.

Deep in the bathroom
a face remains
in the peeling mirror, unregarded,
not my face but the face of a traveller years ago,
trapped there, aging with the rooms
in the vacant forest,
                    the forest with a vacancy.

Voices of frogs, the last frogs, rasp in the night—
they expand and contract, clanking their metal throats.
There is a diastole and systole to the frogs,
last guttering of their mighty race.

I lie down
    and the cold blanket settles around me.
You, author of my exile, think of a black
forest without history—car keys
sealed in a shadow (with toothbrush and pyjamas)
deep in the rock of a forgotten batholith:

There is a dollhouse in *Fachwerkbau*
    strewn among the amplifiers,
there are springs in the overdrive,
    the band is gothic.
The lamps on the walls have mouths,
    they have no words to speak,
the moths have no advice, nor the
    moss on the sidewalk gleaming.
There are wristbones in the gravel
    erupting out of the worn land,
the trees are trailertrash letting the dog out,
    their stained housecoats flap in the wind.

Moths swarm like gods to the smoke of a sacrifice,
    their bodies cigars with magazine covers for wings,
their shadows retain your fingerprints,

and here is Shakyamuni, emitting light from his sodium underbelly,
inscrutable, reducing all to hollow shadows, shadows of
weak gods when they emit so little light. O

author of my exile.

Scene 5: *Dream Pantomime*

The grey light so confabulated there were eels in it swum up from the
    lake—bare tricks of light squirming like invisible and giant tortellini
    under the lamp, twisting migranously beneath the visible. Field
    distortions. Visions chokingly thick in the half-light—O Hildegard—
    your dream city in miniature—its labyrinths and castellations floating,
    swimming! The Superior Sea, the submerged lettering on the black of
    their T-shirts, the car stuffed with clothes and books. A can opener. A
    sewing kit.

There were Black Forest hams
and Black Forest scams,
there were Black Forest cakes
and Black Forest lakes,
there were Black Forest Inns
and Black Forest Djinns.
As they hovered under the lamp
you could almost see them.

<u>Renvoi:</u>
Prince, however foul might body be,
in its covered spaces, curl of your
mouldering cock disincornifistibulated,
snailsnout festering in the flab of a lint-gathering crevass,
retaining stench peroneal from membranes herniated,
fistulae foetid or necrotic in your jiggling ass,
the foxnose of your sweating nipples nodding to the
slumped stretch of your dimpled golf shirt.

Even so is your soul, your hidden essence,
quiddity, hypostasis
as you have made it,
vastly more nauseous, more corrupt, more sick.

Spontaneous Generation: Duplicating Louis Pasteur's Experiment with Modern Apparatus

Today in the domed auditorium left then right and
right again and down the corridor
at the end of the history, Nature
has been absorbed by Capital, pulsing feverishly
in its
endless ascending spiral.

Yet just as Newtonian physics continues its hold
on the bright tangible daytime world, so too
do Aristotle's generations pursue
largely unperturbed
their intuitive quotidieneity.

Studio d'artiste

Shut up alone in an uncontaminated studio, aethereal
particles line-dance across the air,

yes, accept that there is much particulate suspended
in the closed room—Tyndall's Apparatus would reveal:
rejection letters, glum faces at writing workshops,
whispered chatter at the cappuccino bar—these
and other materials, generally toxic,
climbing the currents over the heating ducts
(with their swan-necked
subterranean attachments), or hovering
above the lamp.

Some of these the necrotic poet inspires.

The glistening sky grows thinner beyond the
window, beyond the desk smelling of
dust and furniture polish,
flat and blank as his imagination.

A painting "Children Playing by the Sea" leans outward
from the wall in its spotless lab coat,
monitoring the medium for contaminants.

Sterilizing agent for the imagination—the swift
deoxygenated current of daily employment, office memos,
disconnection notices, relentless restructuring,
while the dissolved sediment of
neo-liberalism erodes the spirit.

*Can stillness here avoid stillbirth? An itch in the clean laboratory
medium—a watched pot which may just boil. Will a tiny flea of excitement
hop, spring out of this sterile sandbar accumulating beside the stream of
global capital? Lyric worms emerge already from the cheesy detritus of the
brain. Night has fallen and a shadow—an eel?—wriggles forth from the
inaugural sparkle of the dew.*

Pasteur, shepherd, this room is an orgy of spontaneous generation , a swan-
necked *Prélude Flasque* to the ever-recuperated commodification of our
bodies, an eddy alongside the all-encompassing current of the late capitalist
day.

Salle d'attente

Left alone in a sealed waiting room
light will spontaneously merge
with darkness, envelop
the photoelectric sensor,
the worsted weave of seat-rows creaking
beneath the aches and coughs of sufferers suffering,
the carpet, hooked up by clumps of sup-hose
to the hoary clientele.
Behind each chair a wallsmudge stained
by years of sad and greying auras.
Acoustic ceiling tiles absorb a sneeze, hanging out,
above the numb beige drywall,
colour-coordinated into
near invisibility.

The panopticon of local illness
reveals all facets of the January malaise,
each laconic gaze raised
and slumping in its turn. Sealed off from the flow of global
capital (even the magazine ads no longer
contemporary), names echo unrecognized,
becalmed outside the universe of productive intercourse.
Lorn of life
lorn of light
lost to a lorn memory long erased.

Waiting here has acquired weight, sinking into a slow Sargasso Sea of itself,
its exposed surfaces devoid even of corporate logos. Tadpoles of ennui
wriggle forth from the carpeted seabed, drawing blank animalcules in
bubbles from the slime. Eels of anxiety emerge, already exhausted,
precipitated from the dew of the room's perpetual night—

Shepherd, this room is an orgy of spontaneous generation, a swan-necked
Prelude Flasque to the ever-recuperated commodification of our bodies, an
eddy beside the all-encompassing current of the late capitalist day.

Chambre à coucher

The room once closed, sealed
but for the swan-necked aperture
opening on the table lamp,
its tungsten filament—incandescing, mediating
a carboniferous jungle ages to the south,
buried beneath the works of years—
heats, emits
photons upon the incarnate solipsism
sterile upon the bed.
Change lies inert upon the dresser, coins
which do not pulse and flow, corpuscles of the
geo-economic body, mere vestigial survivals,
blank eyes staring into the sterile dark.

But in the sealed environment, lifeless forms
quicken, the air ripens
into a haze of suspended pomegranate,
the dry sweetness
absorbed through her porous skin.
Molecules cook in the electrical pool of his spine,
ionized by tactile charges to recombine
in long sticky carbon chains
enlacing and gluing the desiccated subjects.
Rose percale, drapes and drapes of it
bloom around them—pleasure (*jouissance*)
has rebelled, refused
to be subsumed
into the continuum of value.
Oh forget the mythology, sleep
deficit (eliminate it! eliminate it!) will easily
ratchet up their stress levels
eliminate any and all productivity gains.

Moment has acquired gentrification, for this is all of little moment, though a mere video camera might suffice to recommodify the event, join again to the throb of the vast, living world. Tadpoles of longing wriggle forth from the seabed, drawing frivolous animalcules in bubbles from the slime. Eels are precipitated from the dew beading on their skin—

Shepherd, this room is an orgy of spontaneous generation , a swan-necked *Prélude Flasque* to the ever-recuperated commodification of our bodies, an eddy alongside the all-encompassing current of the late capitalist day.

Parc National

The green staircase on the highway map
delineates the space,
Sapir-Whorf hypothesis applied to the
semiotics of land, a frame to hold up
in front of the scene, to look through and
construct the *picturesque*, tuck it away
    in a borderland of marginal economic utility.

Earth emits a corona of grasshoppers
bouncing off the plate glass of my jacket
while the wind, the uninhalable wind
a long wisp-trail of cloud, pilot-whales onto
the waves of land,
shorn nubbin thrones and
dimple vales of sand.

Cry me a gomphothere on the man mouth steppes,
rivets of glaciers in the pocked fuselage
falling away in the antlered sun,
the livid sun,
ghastly scullion
cooking bloodily on the tortured land.

It, it, it is radiant with radiation, beaming upon Grasslands of brown devoid even of fairways—grazing land for insects and bull snakes, unfit for the tourist with not even a last resort (for heaven's sake!). But between shattered windshields of gypsum the sterile seabed emits tiny lizards of wonder even in the absence of invested endospores, dissolving grit has filled your hair with butterflies, and, in precipitate from your wind-born tears scallops of history squirt from your footsteps—

Shepherd, this place is an orgy of spontaneous generation , a swan-necked Prélude Flasque to the ever-recuperated commodification of our bodies, an eddy alongside the all-encompassing current of the late capitalist day.

Envoi: Lined up Before the Ticket Window of Night

Peering through the thin membrane that has formed on the top of your bowl of chicken feet soup, you are unnerved by shadowy movements below the surface. Suddenly you are not yourself: you are the moon, an old woman with fluttering cotton lace teeth, sailing precariously among the chimneys and TV antennas of the village. You are driving a grey North American car filled with cut sticks through a dark residential area where no one lives, only their heating bills steaming up into the sky. A little girl is standing by the side of the road wearing the wedding dress the moon wore at her last wedding. It is much too big for her and smells of mothballs. Mutated elm trees creep over the surface of the road trying to avoid your headlights, they make a popping sound as you drive over them. You want to stop and help the little girl but you can't reach the passenger door because of the sticks, and anyway there is nothing you can do since you are lost too. An enormous snow-covered spruce tree blocks your path. It is the surface of the moon, your skin, which grew up overnight in front of the entrance to the garage. You are moving quite quickly across it, as if on skis, though any sound you make is muffled by the windshield so that movement and stillness are almost indistinguishable. This moon is in fact shining through a blue panel in a stained-glass window in St. Mary's Church in Banff. The panel depicts Our Lady of the Snows—moose and caribou gathered around the crèche, part of a National Geographic *television special on late medieval architecture. You have brought gifts for the baby Jesus but cannot reach him, blocked by the glass he is made of.*

Notes on the Text:

Agaricus and *coprinus* are two genera of fungus. Agaricus includes the common cultivated mushroom. *Mycelia* are the body of a mushroom which grow generally underground, even in the absence of the fruiting bodies. *Nyctanthous* is the tendency of some plants to bloom at night.

Fredric Jameson's essay "Spatial Equivalents in the World System" appears in *Postmodernism, or, the Cultural Logic of Late Capitalism* (Durham, NC: Duke University Press, 1991).

Fachwerk, or *Fachwerkbau*, is the style of building found in Germany and Humboldt, Saskatchewan, in which wooden beams are visible outside the building. Spaces between these beams are filled in with plaster.

Hänsel und Gretel, the opera, is by Engelbert Humperdinck, with libretto by Adelheid Wette. It is set in the mythical forest of Ilsenstein and is less stark than the version of the story in Grimm. The witch's house is surrounded by a fence made of children she has turned into gingerbread in her oven. They are restored to life at the end.

The number of stations in the Roman Catholic "Way of the Cross" was not fixed until the eighteenth century. I have selected ten stations freely from the fourteen of the traditional version and fifteen of the revised version, and have created my own liturgical format by combining the biblical reading and prayer of the revised version with the exhortatory readings of the traditional version, which all begin "Consider..." The description of Ontario Hydro's policy of water flows at Kakabeka Falls is found material. *On the Road* is by Jack Kerouac

Fr. Leonardo Boff, OFM, is a Latin American theologian who has been associated with liberation theology. My treatment of him as a character is completely spurious.

Passagenwerk is the German title of Walter Benjamin's *The Arcades Project* (Cambridge: Harvard University Press, 1999). The image of a bridge between planets and iron ring around Saturn (a balcony in the original) is from excerpts referring to the caricaturist and illustrator Grandville, pseudonym for Jean-Ignace-Isidore Gerard (1803-1847), in the same book.

Louis Pasteur designed an experiment to test the ancient theory of spontaneous generation. It involved enclosing a sterile medium in a swan-necked flask which was open to the air, in order to see if living organisms would arise spontaneously out of non-living material. The theory held that fleas were generated out of sand, worms from cheese, eels from dew, etc. as in the poem.

The Sapir-Whorf hypothesis, which is not accepted by most linguists, posits that particular structures in different languages shape the mental categories of speakers of these languages.

Thanks to:

Don McKay
Tim Lilburn
Jan Zwicky
Sue Sinclair
Peg Evans
Lisa Chisholm
Neal Evans
Bert Almon
Alan Richards
Jennifer Eagle
Ann Stevenson
Hilary Clarke
Robert Currie
Paulette Dubé
Liz Philips
Shelley Sopher
Notes from the Underground
Julie and Stacy Atter
Rhea Tregebov
Sage Hill Poetry Colloquium
Erin Mouré
Dennis Lee
Doug McCarthy
Brad Martin

Thanks to the Saskatchewan Arts Board, the Canada Council and the City of Regina for vital and critical tactical support.